LUNAR LAMENTS

ZAHRA NOOR AWAIS

Printed: June, 2024
Edition: 1st
ISBN: 978-969-749-287-9
Price: Rs 1500 PKR, $10 US

www.auraqpublications.com | raabta@auraqpublications.com
@AuraqPublications | @AuraqBooks | +92-300-0571-530
Printed and Bound by ***Passive Printers*** - www.passiveprinters.com

"There is a moon inside every human being, learn to be companions with it"

-Molana Jalaluddin Rumi

To Abbu Jee, you never left, you live in me
and my book.
To my Palestinian family, always in my heart.

Contents

The reality of life

The colorful life
The faithful sadness

The awful experiences
The impactful memories

The respectful relationships
The mirthful laughs

It's sorrowful.
yet beautiful

When I wished Doom

Shatters everywhere in the room
No piece of heart left to bloom

The threads are all loose on loom
Alone, I cried with the moon

Believing people were nothing but gloom
It pains how I wish doom

Everything Goes

Like a train down a trail
Everything goes

Like darkness terrors to morning smiles
Everything goes

Like waterfalls
Everything goes

Like moments in life
Everything goes

The Pieces of me

Everyone said it's okay
But a piece of me died

They said it'll be over before I know it
But a piece of me died

Sadness won't prolong, I heard
But a piece of me died

Claimed it was only a comma in my sentence
But a piece of me died

The sentence had no room of extension it was a full stop
So, piece by piece whole of me died

All left was a moving skeleton with flesh around it
Without anyone knowing the soul in me died

Me

To me,

Deepest pits of your own thoughts
Decoratively, you survive

Murmurs of others
Screams of hollow

His Mercy

I stood beneath the meteor of mercy
Felt it penetrate right through me

His clemency is unexplainable
But when the droplet landed on my hand

I be anchored that He loves me the most
He will never leave me stranded alone

The One

Stood there in the unknowingness of bounties
An amalgamation of His love

He knew everything
But He heard the sobs

Lost amid worldly desires
Neglected The One who loves

Eid without him

The door I ran to
The place he hugged me

All vacant of love
Left only, the threads of souvenirs

He visits me in trance
But only worth a glance

The eyes on verge of tears
The heart, ice cold of sorrows

Oscar Wilde

"An Irish poet and scriptwriter, popular in the 1880s. He wrote many plays popular back in the day and even now. This poetry is inspired from his quote
"To live is the rarest thing to do""

To live is the rarest thing to do
We may exist but survives who?

Like the lunar eclipse after year
Few and far between

Like a blood fall in the valley
Sparse and gone

It's funny to think
To live is the rarest thing to do

You

You are the warmest jacket
In my coldest nights

Your past is what
I am proud of

Your future is what
I am holding on

The Unanswered Questions

How many times did you die?
How many moments broke you?

How many people became unknown?
How many belonged for you

How many alleviated your fatigued soul
How many were merely shatters for you

How many times did you live?
How many trails it took to find you

Beauty of living

The ineptitude of life
The grace to live
The calm to survive
The storm of grieve
The quake of die

Unexplainable Happiness

The vision of color
The smell of water

All feels enchanting
When I stand there

The peace it radiates
The feeling it allows

The negatively positive

The misunderstood villain
The overexposed hero

A villain kills to protect
A hero dies to survive

Both lay on the same battlefield
Lowest volumes of air passing in

Regret seeps through the hero
Whilst the villain exhales

The hero struggles to live
The villain dies in peace

The love you give me

I love you is an understatement
Words are speechless to say

I admire your eyes
And the universe that settles within them

I admire your face
And the peace it radiates

I admire your lips
And the assurance it gives me

I admire your being
And the love you give me

Shadows within

It's not what we think
the shadows within

The darkness I owned
Was mine from the start

I knew, midnight was the dance round
the forgotten melody is nowhere around

So, to a soulless song
with rhythm I move along

The hide and seek of love

The way we sync in laughter

And when you see my unseen tears

How are you the person you became?
So mesmerizing, got no one to blame

I fail to search your art
The meaning of your heart

The moon is beautiful, isn't it?

Darkness of my own heart
Lightens up when you're around

Oh, how much I want to say
But no word makes it way

I may never say,
Hoping you would know

The masquerade of emotions, isn't it?
Yet the moon is beautiful, isn't it?

Dearest sister,

There are no comparisons
You are an inevitable miracle

I sit there watching you in anger
I admire Even the slightest of you

You are the warmest blanket
You are the deepest secret

Your happiness is all I yearn
Your smile enlightens the house

The knot of ribbon

The knot of ribbon
Tied up firmly

The knot of ribbon
Folds out easily

The knot of ribbon
Straightens simply

The knot of ribbon
Decorates beautifully

The knot of ribbon
Shreds dreadfully

The Leaf and the Tree

The leaf finally falls off the tree
The tree never wanted it
Its branches never owned it

The leaf questions
The tree answers
Blaming it on weathers

Spring flies in
The tree went to hunt
The leaf has left, the tree wonders

The leaf lies lifeless
In the valley

Enduring stomps
"If only my tree knew me"

The deafening silences

The deafening silences
Some die
Some try

The will to strive

I stand and walk again
Even if I fall again

I'll wait for me again
Even if I leave me again

I'll be again
Even if I cease again

The unheard shatters

A sigh of heaviness
A picture of unknown

Breaks the glass
But frame intact

The shatters are in feet
The Pains are not hurt

The Moon Follows

You fall back
And it waits

You walk
And it follows

The people who left will never be back
But trust me, the moon follows

Life is too…

Life is too short to fight back
So just put your gear down

Life is too long to cry over
So just put your smile on

Life is too fragile to lose
So just hold on

Life is too crazy
So just sit back and enjoy the ride

Fool of you

Sparkling or dull
Please let me be me

Laughing or crying
Please let me be me

Self is lost to the void
Oh, fool of you thinking I live being me

Yet I am alone

When the world goes silent
I stand there

Whispers of my sighs
No one's seen yet I stand there

I knew all long
I would be left all alone

What about me

We are one you say
Then go off laughing with others

I stand dumbfounded
I stand there envious

Unable to process
Trying to wipe off the tears you gave me

Glad you are happy
But what about me?

Isn't it lovely?

The way you tell me I will be fine
It's lucky

The way you laugh at my lamest jokes
It's timely

Oh, the way you love me
It's lovely

She is the woman

She is a mother
She is a daughter

She is the one against the odds
She is the one to flourish lots

She is a fearless doom
She is the topic of the room

She is a nameless crown
She is the woman

The serene morning

The morning light seeps in
I sit there, watching

The curtain of orange
Slowly penetrating the white

Unable to comprehend the beauty
I admire from afar

Need

Smiles revealed the row of white, even teeth
A misty layer of darkness beneath

No one saw the tears of hopelessness
A house but homelessness

The immortality of grief
Only necessitated for relief

Once the page turns

And the sun
In my darkness
Rose again
Revealing another page

I sighed believing
It was worth to live
Worth to survive

Smile it off

Today darkens
Tomorrow shines
And the shining tomorrow
Isn't so far for you
To not smile

It's all the same

Opening the door yet again
It was the same place
Same roof
Same floor

There was a difference
Unnoticed
The darkness was gone
It was all clear and shine

The moment it changed

The dull nights
Finally came to an end
The sad faces
Finally smile again

The sad tears
Are finally
Gone for good

He plans the Best

And when you open the door
There will be the unexpected
Because everyone plans
But God plans the best

I lost me

It wasn't pick and choose
It was made for you

It wasn't bright
It was a blind

It wasn't me
It was a soul

that was lost by me

in the haze of me

The filled void

The peace of my house
The screams of my mind

The birds that chirp in the dazing light
The breeze that passes through me

My mind is a ruckus of chatters
My heart is thumping, scared.

All so full
All so empty

Unsure of happenings

The stares are scary
The expectations can kill me

Trying to stitch them
It's a wingless bird

It will devour me
Or it may adore me

The art of immortality

He lives in me
I smile for him

He may have left
But I laugh for him

And when I wipe your tears
I wipe for him

He lives in me
I smile for him

Me and you

I miss the time we were us

You were a loud silence

And I was a thundering lover

My unknown muse

My muse is my dark nights
That I try to enlighten

My muse is my mother's smiles
That I try to enlarge

My muse is the tiny stars
That I see from afar

My muse is the empty sky
That I feel is mine

The bloom of my flower

You are the flower
I never wanted to own
But you bloomed on me
Like you never wanted to go

The immense feeling of love

Love is overrated
I feel tranquil in your eyes

I'm with you
I forget the world

You are the petal of a rose
That I would treasure

Even if you wither and fall
I'll keep you hanging at my wall

Nothingness

When you finish a book
and stare at the wall

When you fake smile
At people you didn't want to meet

When you look
In darkness of your own self

Rain

The droplets on glass
The feeling of happiness

I ran around
Dancing in the rain

The moment healed me
The child in me smiled

My people

The smell of fresh flowers
The immaculate feeling

These people around me
But all I feel is this amity

The emotions of love
And the smiles of my people

What am I?

Throat dried out
I'm worn out

I'm a piece of cloth
Left all alone in the storm

I'm a tingle the heart feels
When it hurts

When the world ends

When it ends
Will I not regret?

When it ends
Will I not cry?

When it ends
Will I see you again?

When it ends
Will all broken be healed?

Home

Home is not you
Home is your smile

Home is your perfectly styled personality
Home is your ability to make me laugh

Home is when you know what I am
Home is your laughs in the echoes

Home is not you
Home is your existing love

The way I love you

You say you hate me
I'll leave you

Tell me to hate you
I'll love you even more

You may never care
My heart yearns you

You are a song
And I wrote the melody

They love

They love,
But they don't know

They love,
But they don’t see

They love,
But they weren't with me

They love,
But they didn't hear the shatters

They love,
But they forgot to love

Smile and tears

The unknowing blow of emotions
The surprising way of me

I sit in guilt
This wasn't in me

I was a smile
How did I end up being the tears?

Rivers of my life

The rivers of my life
Flow so heavily
Flow so elegantly
I never knew they kept me alive in them
All I remember are the moments that pained me

The disturbance of sound

Loud music echoed
They were merely heard

The melodies of grief
Only thing entering

Mind corrupted
Heart disrupted

Your eyes

I look in them
They are decorated with stars

You hold universes in them
I'll admire them with my heart

How can you look in the mirror?
Are you not mesmerized?

I look and I forget
The world isn't moving

It stops.

My flower

I zone out on my own thoughts
I stand there looking in the deep orbits

There were once a few minutes
When I had a blooming flower

I cared for it
I watered-down

It ended down my feet
Without the realization

You left

You left, so who will tolerate raging self?
You left, so who will care about me?
You left, so who will live with me?
You left, so who will love me?
You left, so now there's none of me left

The joy of loneliness

Sit alone in the empty
Feel the world pass you

The joy in being alone
The peace of a noiseless mind

I wonder if I am happy
Who cares at least I dance on my song

One soul down

I write today, tomorrow and tonight
to let my words know
they aren't alone like every night

People are blind when I write
deaf when I speak
mute when I ask

Am I the problem or the solution now?

Pretend that you care

I know nothing matters
I know what you never were

So, I don't care
But I wish you would

No one cares
But I pretend you care

Everlasting melodies

The never-ending dance
The rhythms of life

I am not giving up
I am moving with the beat

Forever swaying with
These everlasting melodies

Feeling of someone

Others may love me
Others may worry for me

But you will save me on my lowest
But you will be by me the longest

I choose happiness

Life gave everything
I choose happiness

People gave inattention
I choose happiness

Out of all the options given
I choose happiness

I may not look like it
I choose happiness

What will happen?

Engulfed with fear
I sit in such atmosphere

Hands trembling
Mixed feeling

What will happen?
Just be a tap in

The contrasting perspective

I feel out of place
Like a sun on midnight

The eyes look at me weird
All needed was a change

Now it impresses
I am special

A unique monument
Of the pains once felt

People are admiring
The person I am now

Where are you?

I left you all alone
Are you lonely?

I seem to smile without you
Are you happy?

Five long times
Where are you?

Just be in peace
They didn't deserve you

Over and over again

The same emotion
Over and over again

The exact place
Over and over again

One thing falls apart
Others follow by it

Over and over again
I fail to feel alive

Heart and mind

Stop thinking about them

But they love?

Stop caring

But they worry?

Stop thinking forever

But they believe?

No one is here now

But they were once?

The will to live

Chatters in my room
Quite in my head

So many selves looking
I feel blind

I'm just done
I just want to survive

Leftover

Moving in rounds
Where will I go?

Barely made it through
Where will this take me?

The itch of voices
Where is the silence?

The leftover life
Please let me survive

Fair cut of life

Twelve at clock
All soundless

I'm waiting for my peace
The world is shut, why am I not?

The ones claim love
I don't see any

But I'm going
I will end up fair

No words left to say

My words are ending
You are so unexplained

Speechless are your eyes
I can't justify their beauty

I apologize I'm unable
To express unavoidable

Sunrise

The clouds glide pass me
The breeze is ice cold

Too invested in songs of birds
I see the sun

It rises up to its full
It looks so tempted to make me fall in love

Everything that ends

Everything that ends
Is a new start

Everything that ends
Is a chapter of love

Everything that ends
Is never really ending

The roads, trees and flower

Roads of my love. Witness.
How I loved every part of you

The trees of the sidetrack, know.
How I ached for your presence

The flowers of my yard, be sure.
How I was fatigued for you

Forget and forgive

I changed in a blink

I'm not what I was

I changed in seconds

I forgive what I was

I changed for you

Now I forgot what you were

The fragrance of love

The giggles of our own
Are the same as they were

The pain in my eyes
Is the same when you are hurt

The jokes you crack
Are the same always

The fragrance of love
Is the same when I met you

The world within our world

Brain is a world of its own
I'm unable to comprehend

It tells me things
Really hard to do

My instincts follow
But my heart remains

Late diagnosis

I was unaware
Of the injury in my heart

I was too late
To treat it now

I was forced to live like it
To let nobody see

Mistake peace

The city calls out to me

I am deaf

The rustling of life urges me to look

I am unable to do so

The unauthorized disclosure

I am sure to ignite

Strategies of nothing

I work for myself

I think I know it all

All I got is emptied

I'm too late

I have attached myself

To unseen strategies of nothing

Sorry to those I love

I'm discarded of care
I'm going to ruin for you

The castle of my own
Is falling apart by me

Sorry to those I love
I'm not living just enough

Let's do it

My anthem is my own pain
I strive through it

So, come along
So, breathe with me

Let's all survive by it
Let's all give the best

Drained already

Emotionally drained
But are emotions good?

I just want to feel something
The same empty-handed heart is pain

Still seventeen

I might be okay
I might do it all over again

But I will never be 17
Having a rush to meet mines

The adrenaline to finish
The anxiety of future keeping me on

We are never alone

I write to feel

At least I feel

It's rare to do

But At least I do

I got my people to get me

You may have no one

But trust me you always got one

Syncing in paining

I wasn't thinking
I was jotting

No one knew what storm settled inside me
When I show I'm too much

When I don't, I'm nothing
So just hold on it's a ride

We are syncing
in the forever aching.

Miss you

Craved so much
I hear your voice

Telling me it's all fine
I know it will be

Scared, I still shiver
The more I think

The more I fall

A gone case

You are in the sky
I sit down in the depths

You know how I do
Am I the only one clueless?

All I wish for
Is your happiness with me or without

The crystal smiles

Smile for me once
Smile for me again

Your smile is keeping me alive
You chuckle when I look

Love wasn't easy
We don't see

You still stay
For me you would always

The extra eyes

Now it may seem easy
You're a routine in my lazy

So don't ever hurt of die
For I am behind thus you may try

And don't think its cliché
Just worried like all other days

I own an extra pair of eyes
To see the future ahead of you after the cries

Thus, my friend it may look weird
But I'm here for the crook to be cleared

Dark betrayals

The pain kicked in
I swallowed my pride

My love for you
Was keeping me alive

Unaware of the fact
You were the one stabbing me in from behind

One day it will be nothing right?

One day tell me
You loved nothing

One day tell me
I cared for nothing

One day tell me
You left nothing

One day tell me
So, I move on of nothing

No goodbyes

Eyes swell up
Tears are tired

I'm still grasping
On our memories

The stars tell me
You are there

I just don't believe
I want to hold you once

See for yourself

You are my words

I write you

You are the moon that follows me

I loved you more than love

I wish I could print out my feels

So, you would know

You are not what you think

If you ever saw, you through me

Start anew

The end is near
But is it really?

I can start anew
I can doodle all over again

Fold up a new page
Begin my own new chapter

Water, fire, air

If I was in the water
Am I the wave or the depth within

If I was in the fire
Am I the flame or the ashes around?

If I was in the air
Am I with you or somewhere unknown?

If I'm still in me
Am I the known or the one unknown by own self now?

With you, a part of me

I remember the faint noises
The loud laughs
The love of years

Wish the time gave me some time
So, I sit and talk till night of nine

I hope you see what I see
For I laugh and smile with you a part of me

Freedom

The chains of fear are heavy
The walls of limitation are high

My screams for freedom were ignored
I was alone in this fight

No place to weep in
No place to laugh out loud

The Shackles

I have dreamed of dreams unstrained
I have hoped for hopes unfouled

I have longed for pursuits untainted
Wait of long, the shackles finally fall

None

I am an unknown cause
A language no one knew

A dish no one liked
A channel all skipped

An old jacket none know about
Like a dreamcatcher in a home of no dreams

Who are you? you ask
I don't know myself

Maybe the colon no one uses
Maybe the moon that brightens from the sun

If you are here

If you are here
You read it all

If you are here
You know it all

If you are here
You went through it all

If you are here
Thank you for it all

Acknowledgements

Well, here we are, it took me 2 years but here we are.

Mama, baba, thank you for making this happen and making me believe I'm no less. My forever baby girl and my always best friend, Thanks for the unhinged editing, Abba Jee. Your support is the reason I was able to get this moment right now, Love you two.

Mimi, EW, but thank you bro. I was able to not lose my confidence and write this all because of you. I'm not going to go all cringe with this stuff but best big support every Lil one needs.

My tkg gang, Shiza and Fatima. The only best friends anyone ever wants. The only people on this planet that know THE Zahra. They are a big part of why this happened. The moment I finished this book I told Shiza; bro had the best reaction. Fatima calling me an author the moment I started lunar laments, you folks are my reason.

MARIAAA!! I did it! You are the best, what else can I say, thanks a lot bro, you deserve the credits more than me, I love this book because of you. Always my best lover!

My 4, who always support me, Zarish, Maria, Shiza, Fatima, this is for you.

Alishba, look what happened? I have a finished book now, I'm not good at words so I hope you know what I feel.

Wins and Fatu!? Zoro did it guys <3.

My grandparents, my muse for everything, my warmest hugs. Thank you.

Lastly, to all those people I feel awkward hugging, this book is a big hug from my end. My family, friends and all those who supported me.

What more can I say, I did it!

Printed and Bound by ***Passive Printers*** - www.passiveprinters.com
Printing press that offers Print on Demand (POD) Facility.
Printed in The Islamic Republic of Pakistan.

www.ingramcontent.com/pod-product-compliance
Lightning Source LLC
LaVergne TN
LVHW041114150826
845673LV00007B/2045